# 50 Ways to Tell
# a
# Redneck From
# a
# Hillbilly:

## *The City Slicker's Guide*

Written by: **Earl O'Kuly**

Edited by: **Kara Wills**

**By The Book 4U Publishing**
Brownstown, IL 62418
*www.bythebook4u.com*

ISBN: 978-0-9836908-8-7

Headings:
Redneck
Hillbilly
City Slicker
Guide
Humor
Differences

**Foreword:**
Are there really differences between a Redneck and a Hillbilly?

You better believe it. Sometimes the differences are glaring, sometimes the differences are subtle, and sometimes the boundaries are crossed between them. Rednecks and Hillbillies can even be related. Go figure.

There are a number of examples about trucks in this book, and you will learn why, even though both groups are into trucks, there are differences. And that's just trucks.

**This book is intended to make you laugh, smile, chortle and chuckle, all the while learning how to tell the difference between Rednecks and Hillbillies. It's worth every penny because it makes sense out of the silliness of country folk.**

Enjoy, Earl O'Kuly

50. Do you know the difference between a Redneck and a Hillbilly?  About 3 teeth  with different shades of yellow and 7 shades of brown.

49. How do you tell which house is which? There's a bunch of old cars, on cement blocks, in front of the Redneck's house; there are goats, chickens and maybe a pig in the Hillbilly's front yard. They smell different too!

48. If the house is a trailer house, it's a Redneck's, if it's a doublewide, it's a rich Redneck's, and if it has a dirt floor, it's a Hillbilly's house. And yes, it is swept a couple of times a week whether it needs it or not.

47. Inside a Redneck's house you're liable to find 2 or more hunting hounds*. Inside the Hillbilly's house you'll find hunting hounds, chickens, and sometimes a pig, usually named Lulubelle.

*This isn't always true because if the wife isn't a true Redneck she will make him keep his dogs outside. Just letting you know. It happens.

46. Both Hillbillies and Rednecks drive trucks. But a Hillbilly's is held together with genuine baling wire*, while a Redneck's is held together with duct tape. . . preferably in camouflage.

45. Both Hillbillies and Rednecks drive trucks.  A Hillbilly drives his <u>for</u> work during the week and to go churchin' on Sunday.  The Redneck drives his <u>to</u> work during the week and to go muddin' on the weekend.

Both know how to work on them, in the yard, in all kinds of weather.

44. A Redneck says, "Let's get the dogs and go coon hunting."

A Hillbilly says, "Let's get the dogs and go fetch dinner."

43. A Redneck cuts down trees for firewood to heat the house. The Hillbilly cuts down trees to build the house and uses the trimmings to heat the house.

42. The Redneck has at least 2 chainsaws. The Hillbilly has at least 3 axes and a couple of crosscut saws. Either way, trees will fall, although with Rednecks they don't always fall where planned. Note: And it hurts like the dickens if one falls on you. That one comes from experience!

41. In the summer you can tell a Redneck from a Hillbilly because the Redneck still has his boots on. For you city slickers, hillbillies don't wear shoes or boots in the summer except churchin' and funerals.

40. If you see a slough (that's a muddy, marshy area for you city slickers) you can tell whether it was a Redneck or a Hillbilly that came through by the tracks. You'll see footprints where the Hillbilly came through feelin' for a big snapping turtle for dinner. You'll see one, 8 to 10 foot wide track, where the Redneck came through with his 4x4 truck muddin'. Of course, if he hits it at better than 50 mph it looks more like a crater than a track.

39. A Hillbilly will have a rabbits foot, a lucky coin, a lucky stone and maybe even a lucky owl's feather. The Redneck will have a lucky shirt, a lucky lure, and a lucky hunting spot.

Both can have a dog that's missing an eye and maybe a leg and with all or part of its tail missing and it's called Lucky.

38.  A Redneck dips snuff from a round cardboard container stuck in his back pocket.  A Hillbilly carries a chaw (a large, rolled up tobacco leaf) with his own special recipe of ingredients inside that he got from his maw, his granny, or maybe his Aunt Bertha on his daddy's side, and that he dittlated (that's modified for you city slickers) just a wee bit.

 If offered a bite of chaw, decline.  You might not die if you do chew it, but you will wish you did! Just sharing what I learned the hard way.

37. If he spits in a cup or an empty beer can, he's a Redneck. If he can spit clear across the yard, he's a Hillbilly.

Note: When talking to either group, wear sunglasses, because if they get mad, Rednecks and Hillbillies will spit tobacco in your eye, and it hurts, it hurts bad! Just sharing.

36. A good Redneck can spit a watermelon seed the length of a picnic table and is proud of it.  A good Hillbilly can spit a seed clear across the kitchen and out the winder (same thing as a window for you city slickers) and doesn't think anything of it.

If you don't believe come by next summer and check out the watermelons growing outside that winder.

35. A Redneck's truck often doesn't have mufflers and the tailpipes come straight up through the truck bed right behind the cab and are chrome. The Hillbilly's truck is loud too, but it's because its muffler and tailpipe have rusted off. Note: What little exhaust pipe there is, well, it's being held up by genuine baling wire.

34. If the truck bed has beer cans in it, it is probably a Redneck's truck. If it has straw, wood chips, and a paper bag with an empty bottle in it, it is definitely a Hillbilly's truck. Those cans and bottles are why they smile and wave a lot.

33. City slickers spit in a spittoon. Rednecks spit in a plastic cup or an empty beer can. If you turn your head before you spit, you're a Hillbilly.

32. If you've ever eaten a possum or raccoon, you're probably a Hillbilly. If you've ever eaten chicken wings so hot you couldn't taste your food for 3 days <u>and</u> you're still bragging about it, you're probably a Redneck.

31. If you get your chicken in a bucket, you're probably a Redneck. If you killed it and plucked it yourself, you're probably a Hillbilly.

30.  If you see someone walking down the hall in a hotel with a six pack and a bucket of chicken going into a room where you can hear the Nascar races on TV, you've probably seen a real live Redneck.

If you see someone cleaning a chicken outside the motel before bringing it into their room to cook it, you've probably seen a real live Hillbilly.

If you see a group of people cleaning chickens in the motel bathtub you are seeing Gypsies.  Move to another motel immediately!  If the smell doesn't get you, they will take your belongings. Just sharing what I know.

29. Rednecks ride horses. Hillbillies ride horses, mules, goats, cows, whatever, doesn't matter, it beats walking.

28. A Redneck can track a buck deer. A Hillbilly can track a buck, tell you what he had for breakfast and how many doe (girl deer for you city slickers) he has been seeing.

27. A Redneck carries a multi-purpose tool and can overhaul a car engine with it. A Hillbilly carries a pocket knife, a pair of pliers and some genuine baling wire and can fix anything.

26. A Redneck drinks beer. A Hillbilly drinks moonshine. Both think they can dance after the partaking of their particular poison. Both are wrong.

25. If you know what chittlins are, you're probably a Redneck. If you eat them with your eggs in the morning you're probably a Hillbilly.

24. A Redneck boy will date fat girls, but doesn't want to be seen with them. A Hillbilly boy will date fat girls, **and** wants to marry one.

That's because it gets darn cold in a drafty log cabin with a dirt floor. It saves on firewood too. This ones from hearsay. Just saying.

23.  Get in a fight with a Redneck and when it's over, he'll probably buy you a beer.  Get in a fight with a Hillbilly and it can turn into a family feud that can last at least 3 generations.

22. Most Rednecks won't walk across the street to the next bar, but will run 5 miles to keep up with their coon hounds.  A Hillbilly will walk 3 miles to check a rabbit snare to see if there's going to be meat for breakfast, but rides the mule to chase the coon hounds, because everyone knows raccoons can run a fair piece, plus, the mule enjoys coon hunting.

21. A Redneck, if it's needed, uses a bit of the wife's corn oil to slick his hair down (his mom's if he is under 30 and still living at home). A Hillbilly uses axle grease, preferably used because it's cheaper, however, a rich Hillbilly uses pure hog lard just because he can afford it.

Note: Anyone that uses anything from Walmart for their hair is getting too big for their britches or is a city slicker! Just telling it like it is!

20. A Redneck uses after shave to hide the smell of gasoline from working on his truck. A Hillbilly covers the smell of gasoline naturally from cow dung from milking the cows. Of course, it's goat smell if the Hillbilly is too poor to have a cow. Note: Poor Hillbillies get less dates because goats can get pretty rank at times. However, for some reason, although these Hillbillies don't seem to notice the smell, they do notice they don't get as many dates at their more affluent cousins.

Note: Just to share, during rutting season (that's mating season for you city slickers), a billy goat will relieve hisself* on hisself to attract a female goat. It sounds gross and stinks even worse than it sounds. Just letting you know, you don't want to go there . . . ever! *That's himself for you city slickers.

19. Rednecks blame the dog for their farts.
Hillbillies just say, "Tree frogs!" Doesn't matter,
they both stink things up pretty bad!

18. Hillbillies use a pocket knife to trim their fingernails. Rednecks use their teeth. Both work.

Note: Remember, regardless of the shades of yellow and brown, Rednecks have 3 teeth more than a Hillbilly. (see #50)

17. A Redneck has found about 10 to 20 uses for a plastic grocery bag. A Hillbilly can't even count to the number of ways he can use a gunny sack. Side note: To a Hillbilly those rough, cloth feed bags make some really good clothes. Not that they are Sunday go to meeting clothes, but good enough for Walmart.

16. Most Rednecks can at least count their fingers and toes.  Most Hillbillies can't.

Note: You city slickers don't want to try to city slick hillbillies because they do know money and have been known to turn the table on you all. You've been warned!

15. Talking about fingers and toes, most Hillbillies have lost more digits than a Redneck. However, this is only a rule of thumb. And yes, that was intentionally punny!!! City slickers like punnies.

14. Most Rednecks have a warped sense of humor, and their favorite line is, "Hey, watch this!"   Most Hillbillies say, "That ain't funny!" That's because they don't want Rednecks to get any more big headed than they already are.

13. Both Rednecks and Hillbillies like practical jokes. (This of course is THEIR definition of practical.) A Hillbilly practical joke usually involves heavy lifting, like, "Let's put Jed's go-to-town buggy on top the barn." A Redneck's practical joke is to lead a cow up at least 3 flights of stairs, knowing it can't climb back down. Both hide across the road to enjoy the fruits of their labor.

12. A Redneck has at least 10 rod and reels with over 100 lures of every shape, size and color, just to be prepared. The Hillbilly has 3 cane poles with real cork corks and knows where to find grubs and night crawlers.

They both think they are the greatest fisherman in the world. They're both wrong.

11. When hunting grubs and worms, a Hillbilly's biggest concern is not dropping the rock or log down onto his toes.  Rednecks are more concerned with not electrocuting themselves with the contraption they built from the arms of the TV antenna and a drop cord (that's extension cord to you city slickers).  They use this 'thing' to shock the night crawlers out of the ground.

Note: This isn't recommended anymore since Big Bubba's cousin Little Scoot almost electrocuted hisself.)

10. If a Redneck owns a tractor, it is usually 10 to 20 years old, but looks good with the brush on paint job he gave it.  If a Hillbilly owns a tractor it is much older because he inherited it from his grandpappy . . . and it's held together with genuine baling wire.  Poor Hillbillies are still using mules.

9. To a Redneck, the world's greatest invention was 4 wheel drive. To a Hillbilly, it was when baling machines went from rope to wire, genuine baling wire, which has over 101 uses around the farm!

Note: The book about these will be coming out as soon as we can find a Hillbilly that can read AND write.

8. Rednecks like to take girls out and fool around. Hillbillies like to take girls out and go spoonin'. Both achieve the same result, "Paw I gotta get married!"

7. At Walmart it becomes difficult to tell the difference between Rednecks and Hillbillies. However, by listening closely, the Rednecks are laughing and making fun of the city slickers in their pajamas and ogling the girls that are showing most of their body.  All the while the Hillbillies are looking at the city slickers <u>and</u> the Rednecks, shaking their heads, mumbling, "Disgraceful!"

Somebody said it wasn't the city slickers wearing the pajamas . . . has to be because Rednecks sleep in their undies and Hillbillies sleep in their long johns in the winter and sleep naked in the summer!  None of them even own pajamas.

6. A Redneck can shoot the head off a squirrel at 50 yards. A Hillbilly can shoot the eye out of a squirrel at 50 yards . . . because he doesn't want to mess up breakfast.

5. A good Redneck reads the bible. A good Hillbilly owns a bible.

4. A Redneck can use the 'F' word and 7 other cuss words as good as any sailor. The Hillbilly, when really mad, can make the words, damn, dang, and darn, sound like swear words.

3. A Redneck wears a leather belt with a belt buckle big enough to use as a platter for a cooked turkey.  For a belt, the Hillbilly is using the rope leftover from the outdated, pre-wire balers because he's saving the baling wire for better uses.  Note: Older Hillbillies have been known to use suspenders, but it was only because they ran out of rope.  Of course, some Hillbillies wear bib overalls because they like to look like farmers.

2. If you ask a Redneck if he is a Redneck, he'll say, "Nope, I'm a country boy." If you ask a Hillbilly if he's a Hillbilly, he'll say, "Nope, I'm a country boy." They're both wrong. A country boy is the guy that owns more than 5 acres, smokes store bought cigarettes, doesn't chew, barely drinks, doesn't go muddin', and definitely doesn't drink moonshine. He sometimes claims to be a Redneck so as to be seen as cool. He never, ever claims to be a Hillbilly, even if he dated his sister once.

**1. And the number one way to tell a Redneck from a Hillbilly is by the ambulance.** You never see a Hillbilly in an ambulance. Hillbillies don't believe in ambulances because Uncle Jed's truck works just fine and is a bunch cheaper.

**As for Rednecks: Ambulances follow Rednecks around all the time because they know, without a doubt, sooner or later someone is going to get hurt. Ambulances know Rednecks! Know them up close and personal. Just saying!**

There it is! Now you have it, the city slickers guide to discerning the difference between Rednecks and Hillbillies.

Now you know so you'll never be fooled again!!!

## If, by now, you think you know your Rednecks and Hillbillies, here are some questions for you:

1. If both the Redneck and the Hillbilly have the same number of guns in the gun racks in the back windows of their trucks and both the Redneck and the Hillbilly arrive at a 4 way intersection at the same time, which one has the right of way? *The Hillbilly because his truck doesn't have brakes.*

2. If the Redneck has more guns in the gun rack in the back window of his truck than the Hillbilly does in his, and both the Redneck and the Hillbilly arrive at a 4 way intersection at the same time, which one has the right of way? *The Hillbilly because his truck still doesn't have brakes, now does it?*

3. What's the difference when a Redneck and a Hillbilly both wear Billy-Bob Teeth? *The Redneck is wearing them to have fun and a real good time. The Hillbilly is wearing them to look good to get a date.*

4. Why does a Redneck go frog giggin'?
*To have fun. Note: Frog giggin' is going out at night with a wooden pole that has a barbed, 3 prong gig on the end of it to catch bullfrogs on the banks of water of ponds and creeks.*

5. Why does a Hillbilly go frog giggin'?
*For dinner when company is coming over.*

6. How can you tell the difference between a Redneck and a Hillbilly when they go to the bathroom? *Most Rednecks have indoor plumbing, i.e., they have a toilet in the house, AND it even works in a rich Redneck's doublewide. Hillbillies still have outhouses. Their motto: If it was good enough for gramps, it's good enough for me! Note: Some Hillbilly folk are no longer using the Sears and Roebuck catalog to wipe with, but are actually putting real toilet paper in their outhouse.*

7. How can you tell the difference between a Redneck and a Hillbilly when they need to pee outside (relieve themselves for you city slickers)? *The Redneck will find the nearest tree. The Hillbilly doesn't, but he does look around to make sure the cow, goats and sheep aren't looking. They're not pets, they're family.*

*City Slicker Score:*
*If you missed 3 or more, for heaven's sake, stay in the city!*
*If you missed 2, be careful where you walk when you're in the country.*
*If you only missed one, you did good.*
*If you got them all right, you probably cheated or you aren't really a city slicker, you've got Redneck and/or Hillbilly blood in you!!! Just saying!*